The Meaning & Power of Covenant in Marriage

Drummond & Lindah Robinson

INTRODUCTION

Perhaps you met as you bumped into each other rushing to work, perhaps you went to a social event, a dinner party that friends invited you to and you connected across the room. Many people have said, "I saw him/her across the room and I knew that was the person I was going to marry, I bumped into that person and knew after five minutes of conversation this was the person for me." There was that spark, the fire of love was ignited, and the passion for each other then grew. There was intense attraction and a commitment of undying love. This love would last forever! Everything was perfect, nothing was wrong! It always amuses us to listen to couples who are about to get married, describing their relationship, how they met and how perfect he or she is.

"this love would last forever... Everything was perfect..."

What happens then to that undying love for each other? Many people say to us, "Well the fire has gone out! I don't feel anything anymore!"

Perhaps you have heard of similar stories to the one we shared. You may even have gone through such a crisis. Maybe your story is not so dramatic but you are in a marriage that has over the years lost its passion, fun and excitement. I can't tell you how many times we've heard these words "we just exist together, mostly for the children. There is no meaningful communication or love. We are like ships passing in the night." The disappointment and hopelessness of that kind of relationship can be very crushing and painful. It is like a slow death of our hopes, dreams, peace and joy. We have realised that marriage doesn't suddenly end in divorce! Toxic seeds that are sown years before begin to bear fruit resulting in a harvest of destruction. The seeds of infidelity and divorce are sown through the way we treat each other over a period of time.

Couples come to us for counseling when there is a huge crisis in their marriage. They can hardly look at each other from anger, hurt and bitterness. We always like to ask them how they met … what attracted them to each other to the point that they realised that they wanted to get married. As they begin to think back, we will begin to see a little bit of a smile reappear on their face, a little bit of a twinkle in their eye as they remember the fun times. They even laugh a little about some of the funny things that happened, sometimes ten, fifteen, twenty-five years ago. They fondly recall what attracted them to each other, and the good times that they shared. Now things have changed, there is resentment, bitterness, betrayal and often times even hatred!

One of the main reasons that the passion of love is lost and marriages breakdown is that couples have no understanding of the meaning and power of Covenant. Lets imagine you were given a brand new Ferrari to drive, with all its power and potential. What a thrill. However, if you do not treat it according to the manual in the way you drive, service and maintain it, even a Ferrari will break down. So marriages are breaking down simply because couples are violating God's manual on marriage. They have no idea how the manual on Covenant should be used and the result is a devastating break down. This could all be avoided. So lets take a look at God's heart for marriage and the Covenant God put in place to protect and enrich our marriages.

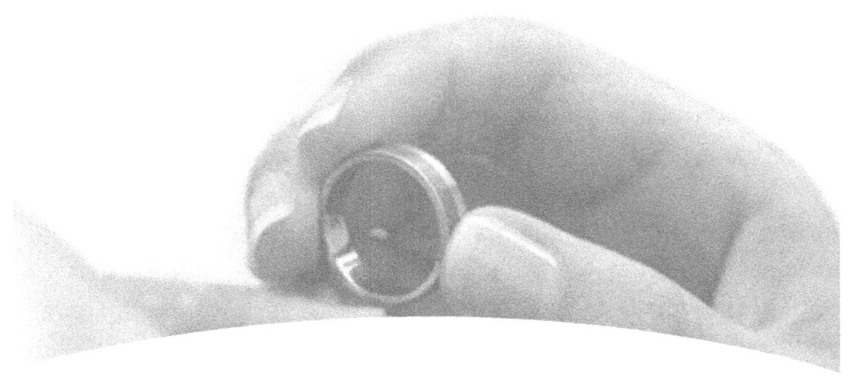

Chapter 1

GOD'S HEART FOR MARRIAGE

Gen 1:26&27

Then God said, "Let us make man in our image, after our likeness. And let them have dominion over the fish of the sea and over the birds of the heavens and over the livestock and over all the earth and over every creeping thing that creeps on the earth." So God created man in his own image, in the image of God he created him; male and female he created them.

Two Key Words Here Are "Us" And "Our".
They speak of a relationship, the divine "Family" of the Godhead. In fact "family" is a word rooted in God. It is a relationship of complete unity, mutual submission and intimacy. A relationship based on Covenant, as Covenant is the deepest form of intimacy that there is.

So God created man and woman to be joined together in the Covenant of Marriage to be a reflection of the divine unity of the Godhead, to live together in harmony, mutual submission and intimacy. From this place of unity, they would be able to rule, reign and have Dominion over the earth. Unfortunately, we see that man has not lived in the purposes and design of God. There is disunity, division, domination, manipulation and as a result, chaos upon the face of the earth.

God designed the Covenant of Marriage to be the central and pivotal structure of relationship in the Kingdom of God and on earth. Our relationship with Jesus is as a Bride to a Groom. Jesus did not come just to "save" us, but to draw us into the covenant of marriage with Him as that is the deepest form of intimacy.

Hosea 2:16-20

> *And in that day, says the Lord, you will call me 'My Husband,' and no longer will you call me 'My Baal.' For I will remove the names of the Baals from her mouth, and they shall be remembered by name no more.*
>
> *And I will make for you a covenant on that day with the beasts of the field, the birds of the air, and the creeping things of the ground and I will abolish the bow, the sword, and war from the land, and I will make you lie down in safety.*
>
> ***And I will betroth you to me forever.***
> ***I will betroth you to me in righteousness and in justice, in steadfast love and in mercy. I will betroth you to me in faithfulness. And you shall know the Lord.***

The Bible is a "love story", a courtship and finally an eternal marriage of Jesus Christ to us, His church.

Rev 19:7-9

> *Let us rejoice and exult and give him the glory,*
> *for the marriage of the Lamb has come,*

How sad it is that mankind has violated this love story, has rejected her groom and husband and mocked the purity and beauty of marriage. Many think that Christianity is about attending church, holding a form of religion that will be a "fire escape" from hell with the hope of somehow making it to heaven. The truth is, that if you don't have an intimate covenant relationship with your groom Jesus on earth, you will not by some default have it in heaven.

When a bride comes down the aisle on her wedding day, she looks lovingly at her husband to be, waiting for her at the altar. It is not someone she has heard about or read about, or seen at a distance. She has kept herself pure and spotless for her love, they have declared their unconditional love for each other and now this union will be sealed in the covenant of marriage, in the deepest from of intimacy, spirit, soul and finally body.

Let's discuss the following diagram,

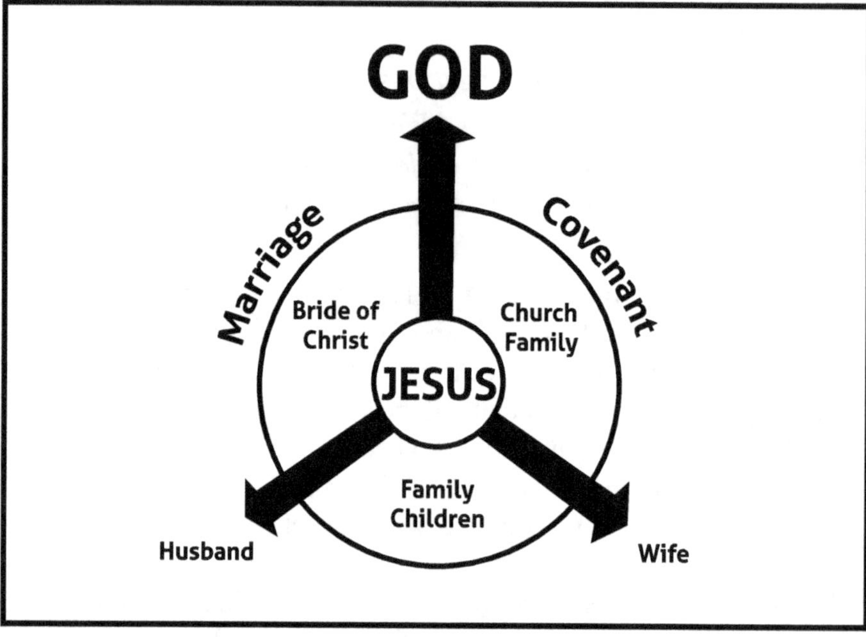

Our relationship to God is through the Covenant of Marriage that
we enter into with Jesus Christ.

The outer circle in the diagram represents that circle of covenant.
In other words, the only way we can come to the Father is through
entering into an intimate covenant relationship with Jesus Christ.
This is one of the most significant differences between Christianity
and all other religions.

Jesus said, no one comes to the Father except through Him,
*Jesus told him, "I am the way, the truth, and the life. No one can
come to the Father except through me. (John 14:6 NLT)*

When we enter into that covenant relationship, we become sons and
daughters of God and part of the Bride of Christ. We are then added

into a local church family where can find fellowship and expression of the gifts God has given us as we serve one another.

I hope you can see how the two covenants are interwoven and find expression in each other. Our marriages are then carried by the anointing and power of the Spirit of this eternal covenant.

We can see how if a husband and wife break their own marriage covenant for no biblical reason, how this can affect their own covenant and intimacy with God. Furthermore, I believe it grieves the heart of God and challenges the very central spirit of covenant each time a marriage covenant on earth is destroyed. This then would be the main aim and plot of the enemy.

Each time a man and woman are joined together in covenant, they enter into the eternal covenant of marriage between Jesus and His church. There is an anointing and empowering of the Holy Spirit to live in the fullness of covenant and the blessing of marriage.

God's heart and purpose is that our marriages would be a reflection of the divine unity of the Godhead and the eternal marriage of Jesus Christ to His bride, the Church.

IT IS NOT OUR MARRIAGE WITH WHICH WE CAN DO WHATEVER WE WANT. MARRIAGE IS ACTUALLY INTRINSICALLY LINKED TO THAT ETERNAL COVENANT.

If the marriage covenant breaks down, the blessing is stolen and all relationships involved suffer. Even our relationship with Jesus can suffer if we stubbornly proceed to destroy our marriage and violate the sanctity and holiness of marriage.

That is why there is such an attack on the sanctity of marriage at the moment. One hundred years ago, 1 in 300 marriages ended in divorce. Today, over 50% of marriages end in divorce resulting in tremendous hurt, rejection, shame, broken lives and families. The devil is attacking that which is closest to the heart of God as we approach the final return of Jesus to attend the Marriage Supper of the Lamb.

When Jesus went to the cross, He paid the price for our sin, took our shame, broke the curse and set us free to once again enter into the freedom and intimacy of covenant with Him. He cut covenant with us by shedding His blood on the cross, releasing mercy and unconditional love towards us. We now have the choice to lay down our lives, and enter into that "LOVE COVENANT" with Him and then reflect the very heart and intimacy of that covenant into our own earthly marriages. The result will be marriages that reflect intimacy, peace, joy, harmony and abundant blessing.

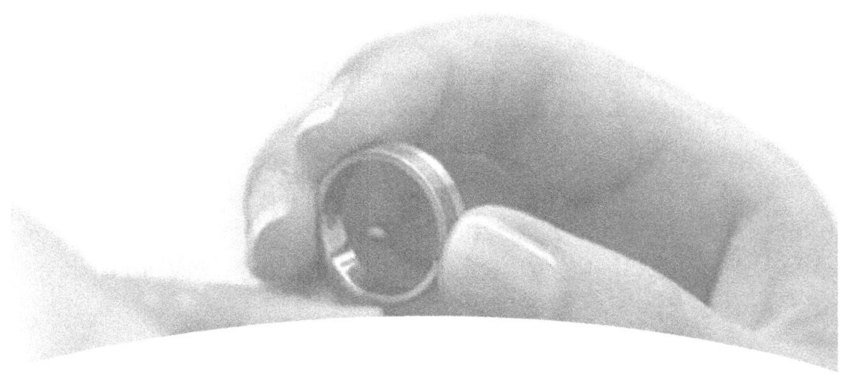

Chapter 2

INTIMACY IN MARRIAGE

Intimacy speaks of total unity, oneness, harmony and connection.
It blossoms and grows when there is total trust, openness,
vulnerability, mutual submission and yieldedness. An intimate
relationship is based on respect and honour, truth and light. In fact
there can be no "darkness", no deceit, lies and shame if true intimacy
is to grow. When a marriage is founded and built on this depth of
intimacy, it truly becomes supernatural, because it is infused by the
Spirit of God. The result is a family living in the favour and blessing
of God.

In Genesis 1:28, it says, "and God blessed them". This "blessing"
means: to be empowered to prosper! To have an abundant sufficiency
and more than enough to share with others. To rule and reign and
govern the earth so everyone will live in peace, prosperity and
favour with God.

Well, we realize that this is not happening around the world. We
see broken families, struggling and burdened people striving for a
small measure of peace, joy and blessing.

The reason is, people do not have an understanding of the meaning and power of covenant. They have no vision and goal for their marriage besides having their own needs met and experiencing selfish pleasure.

So lets examine what "covenant" is and how we can begin to enter into an intimacy that can literally transform our lives, marriages and families.

Covenant brings us into intimacy, where there is total vulnerability, harmony and knowing one another, spirit, soul and body. This kind of intimacy cannot develop through a casual acquaintance!

It also cannot develop when the other person is always threatening to leave. That breaks trust, vulnerability and intimacy.

We were doing a talk for a radio station, and made the mistake of inviting people to call-in with any questions. We were talking about intimacy and many people phoned in. Someone said, "Well, I've had sex with my boyfriend. Have I now come into a place of intimacy from God's perspective? Have we become one flesh?" My answer was No! The kind of sex she had didn't bring her into one flesh - it brought her into a lot of trouble - in fact a "curse".

It requires much more than that to come into that place of intimacy that Jesus was speaking about when he said, *I have given them the glory that you gave me, that they may be one as we are one - I in them and you in me - so that they may be brought to complete unity. (John 17:22,23 NIV).* The kind of intimacy that Jesus was expressing in this verse, was where he and the Father are one in each other, and that he desires us to have the same kind of intima-cy. Well you can have that kind of intimacy only by entering into covenant.

Now, Jesus made a way for us to come into intimacy with the Father, by cutting covenant with us; that is, by giving his life on the Cross. His blood was shed, because covenant is always sealed by the shedding of blood. Because of God's great love for us, he entered into a blood covenant with us through Jesus Christ, giving his life on the Cross, and all who will, may then enter this covenant. But it is only through covenant that we receive the life of Christ and intimacy with God.

Well if it's only through covenant, then we need to understand what covenant is. So let me give you a brief description of covenant. **Covenant is the most solemn of all contracts. It is irrevocable; indissolveable, and it is a commitment valid until death, and covenant is sealed in the shedding of blood.**

Now there's another important aspect here, and you need to get this; covenant does not depend upon the performance of the other party, or the other person you are entering into covenant with. Because when you cut covenant with them you give yourself totally to them, irrespective of whether they perform back or not - that's covenant.

Well if that's covenant, what is contract?

Contract is the a bi-lateral agreement between two parties to fulfil certain conditions and so very dependent on the performance of either of the two parties. If one party fails to perform the other party can cancel. For instance, if you order a new red car, and you go to collect at the time given to you; but when you get there, it's a white car, what are your options? The salesman says, "sorry, we didn't have red, but it's the same car, everything is exactly the same, it's just that it's white." Well, you are not obliged to fulfill that contract – you can cancel that contract because they have not fulfilled the conditions of the contract.

The problem is that the world sees marriage as a contract; but marriage is not a contract, marriage is a covenant. So let's have a look at what the key elements of covenant are.

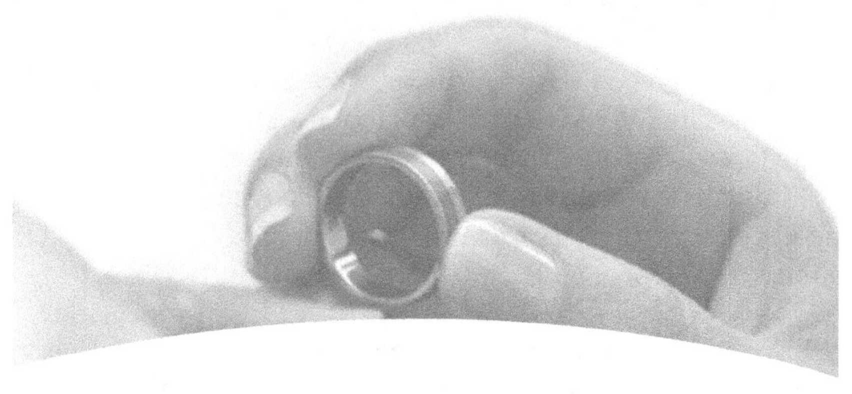

Chapter 3

THE ELEMENTS OF COVENANT

We see in Genesis chapter 15 how God cut covenant with Abraham. God knew the way people would cut covenant in those days. If two people wanted to enter into covenant with one another, they went through the kind of steps we're going to describe.

God said to Abram, *"Look towards the heaven, and number the stars, if you are able to number them, so shall your descendants be."* So God made this incredible promise to Abram that his descendants would be as numerable as the stars. But in verse 8 Abram says, " *Oh Lord God how am I to know that I shall possess all this?"* and God said, *"Abram, bring me a heifer, three years old, a she goat, a ram, a turtle dove, and a young pigeon,"* and he brought them all to the Lord, and he cut them in two and laid each half over against the other... and as the sun was going down a deep sleep fell upon Abram, ... "when the sun had gone down it was dark, and behold a smoking fire pot, and a flaming torch passed between those pieces of flesh, and the Lord made a covenant with Abram saying 'to your descendants I will give the promises that I have made to you'". (paraphrased from Genesis 15:5-17)*

You see, God understood and knew the way that they made covenant in those days. So I think it's important for us to go through some of these steps of covenant to see how Jesus fulfilled each element when He cut covenant with us on the cross and how these steps apply to our marriage vows and covenant.

1. Exchanging Of Robes

The first thing two people would do if they wanted to cut covenant is that they would take off their robe and give it to one another. Now their robe was not just a piece of clothing that they bought at their local store. It had very significant meaning. A robe was a certain colour, it had certain tassels on it, it had certain coloured beading on it, and their robe signified some very important things about that particular person. If you saw a person you could immediately identify their position, their title, their reputation, and who he was in the community. You could see that he was head over a particular family or tribe. Just looking at his robe told the whole story about the person. So for someone to take their robe off and give it to somebody else, he was literally giving away his whole life. You see it wasn't just a piece of clothing; it was the title to all that he was. Okay! So they would swap those robes, and say, "All that I am, my whole life, I give to you."

Now when Jesus went to the cross, He also exchanged robes with us. He took our garment of shame and sin and gave us His robe of salvation and the garment of righteousness. He gave us His whole life, we became joint heirs with Him, seated with Him at the right hand of God in a place of honour and authority. He set us free from an orphan spirit and brought us into sonship.

When we get married, we do not actually swop robes (the bride would not want to give up her wedding dress) but in our hearts, that is actually what we are doing and saying. "All that I am, I now give to you, my rights, title, position, wealth and heritage".

2. Exchanging Belts

The second thing they would do is that they would exchange belts. On their belts hung their weapons; their sword, dagger, shield etc. As they swapped belts they were saying something very important. "From now on your battles are my battles." My belt represents my strength, my armament, my ability to fight a battle. I now give you my armament, strengths and abilities; "Whenever you get into a battle situation, call on me and I will be there. It doesn't matter when it is; 365 days a year – I will be there. Midnight on Sunday night, I will be there."

Jesus gave us his strength to cover our weaknesses - like the exchanging of belts. He says, *"Now your battles are my battles,"* Romans 8:37 says that, *"we are now **more** than conquerors through Christ Jesus,"* **more** than conquerors - where we are weak He is strong; I can do all things through Christ Jesus who strengthens me. That's a great exchange! That we have surrendered our weakness for his strength, and his ability.

Now, in our marriages, because it's a covenant we too have exchanged "all". Our strengths and our weaknesses; our abundances and our lacks; in every area we have exchanged everything. In covenant you come alongside to strengthen each other in the challenges we face on a day to day basis. It's not a matter of saying, "I'm sick and tired of your weaknesses; I'm just tired of fighting your battles, and I don't want to be in this covenant any more."

As I have said, that is not possible, because if you do not fulfill the terms of your covenant you could come under a curse. Perhaps that is why people around the world are facing such massive struggles and challenges. You are there to meet those weaknesses and to strengthen them in their time of need.

On a personal note, I know that when we got married, we faced some major adjustments. I had been in the Navy for my one year military training. In the Navy you live on a ship, and in the ship they give you a tiny box for all your personal clothes, etc. Your shirts have all got to be perfectly ironed, and perfectly packed, your socks folded in a perfect circle placed in a row, everything is exactly in its right position.

Then we got married! I came to realise that Lindah had a different approach to packing and cupboards. She would come to the cupboard and sort of push everything in, and if necessary, lean against the door and lock it. Because we lived in a very small apartment, sometimes we had to share the same cupboard! So all my things in a neat row suddenly became pushed aside so that Lindah's stuff could be pushed in there. Now, she's not like that anymore, and I know this doesn't happen to you, but this is one of the things that happened to us.

The other thing that we kind of had to work through was that, my wife is a wonderful cook! In fact I'm sure she's the best cook in South Africa! When Lindah cooks, she cooks with a passion. Now what I mean by passion is that Lindah goes into the kitchen and thinks, "I'm going to cook a meal for my husband, and for my family, that is the best meal in the world!" Now in her passion, I don't know why, but she thought she had to use every pot and utensil in the kitchen. She would pull out all the drawers, and put every pot on, and then go to the glassware pots and put them on to. Then she would mix a little bit of this, and then a little bit of that, and soon all the utensils were used and dirty.

I kind of lived with this for a while, and then I said, "Now, look Lord, we've got a problem here, we've got a serious problem here. My wife is a wonderful cook, but she has a weakness you know. She's just a little bit untidy; Lord, could you change her because she really needs changing!. Thank you Father."

You know, Lindah didn't change, so I prayed a little bit harder, and

eventually I had to do serious business with the Lord, and the Lord said, "Actually Drummond, we've got a bit of a problem here."
And I said, "Yes, there is a problem. Lindah's untidy and you
        need to change her."
And he said, "No, you're the problem."
        I said, "No, I'm not the problem Lord, you don't understand, my wife has a problem, can you please change her?"
        "No, you're the problem, because you don't understand covenant."
I said, "Well, what do you mean by covenant?"
 "Well covenant means, that where Lindah is weak, you are strong - you cover her weaknesses."
        "Oh well that sounds nice, so what does that mean?"
"Well it means that you help her by washing the pots and dishes
        and clean the kitchen!"
I said " is there anyone else up there I can talk to!"

So that's what I had to learn to do. And so I said, "Okay, I'll do that Lord," and I went in there and I washed a couple of pots and dishes, and put them back in the cupboard, nice and clean. But as soon as they were back in the drawer she took them and used them again!

We all have differences and challenging situations in our relationships. Sometimes this causes confrontation and eventually we say, "I can't handle this weakness anymore; I don't know if I can tolerate it anymore; I've absolutely had enough. Unless you change, I'm out of here. Well to have that kind of mentality, let me tell you, is not to understand covenant; because in covenant you come alongside one another and serve each other! I learned to help her and we got on happily ever after. You see, Lindah also covered a lot of my weaknesses; I mean just in the area of cooking, if Lindah hadn't done the cooking I'd have eaten scrambled egg from then until now because I am useless at cooking. That is a lot of scrambled egg!, So she covers my weaknesses there and she covers my weaknesses in many other areas. She's very creative and I'm not that creative. As

I say, I'm very orderly, but she's creative.

Pins and Needles

Lindah would sew huge banners, so big you could not put them on the table because it was not big enough. So she put them on the bedroom floor, between the wall and the bed, covering the whole floor. Lindah would do these banners and I would say, "Wow, this is wonderful darling. How long is this going to take? Is this like a day or two!" As the whole vision and creativity evolved, Lindah would use one box of pins and then another box of pins, and about four boxes of pins later, and a month into this whole project, I faced some challenges. On a good day, I would get into bed with only two pins in my toes! On a bad day, five pins in my toes! And so these things test you, but when the banner goes up on the wall of the church I would say, "Hey look at my wife - she made that banner, isn't she wonderful?"

She has brought much creativity into our home and ministry, which would otherwise be so boring, because I'm just not like that. I don't make beautiful things for our home, but she does. That's how we compliment and complete each another.

We exchange our strengths and our weaknesses; and that's what covenant is all about, it should always be like that and it should never end. You mean, if Lindah still keeps pulling out the pots and things like that then you keep covering her? Well, yes, that's covenant. Because, you see, when we got married, we said, "My strength will cover your weakness." Now of course we should not take advantage of one another. Because you love each other, you should have a desire to please each other. In our desire to please one another we try and protect one another from feeling used. The truth is there will always be areas of weakness that you can get uptight about, but if you understand covenant then you approach it in a whole new way. You say, "God that's why you put us together! So that our strengths can compliment one another and we can come alongside each other to strengthen one another in the challenges we face, on a day to day basis.

3. Animal Sacrifice

Then they would seal the covenant with a sacrifice, much as was described in Genesis 15. They would take an animal, cut it in half, and split the pieces apart with enough room to walk between them. They would stand back to back in the middle of the pieces, and they would proceed to walk a figure of eight in the blood and around the two pieces of flesh until they then came together again facing each other. Then they would say, "If I ever break this covenant, let the same be done to me, as has been done to this animal." Also, of course, there blood was all over the place, signifying that this covenant was now sealed in blood. They had in a sense, died to self so that the new covenant could be established.

 You may have read how in some cultures they would then cut a slit in their wrist and mix their blood together. Once healed, there would be a scar that had very significant meaning because it was visible to others.

The scar was quite significant, because if you were living in a tribe and you cut covenant with the tribe next door to you, and you went on a trip, and were confronted by someone who wanted to attack you, you could raise your hand and they would see your covenant scar. They would know that you had cut covenant with somebody, and they would have to be far more cautious about attacking you because they knew that if they attacked you, whoever you had cut covenant with would come and attack them. So they would respect that and think, "Whoa, let's first talk to this guy and find out who is behind him, it might be somebody much stronger than we are," That was the significance of the scar. It is told that when Livingston and Stanley went into Africa, they cut covenant with the first tribe they encountered and that this became their protection as they travelled deep into Africa.

On reading literature on different people groups that performed these covenant ceremonies, I discovered something incredible. If a person cut covenant with somebody and then broke that covenant, they would hunt him and even his family down for up to three or four generations and kill everyone. So the bottom line was basically that you did not break covenant. I think that if we had that kind of covenant ritual today, we wouldn't have too many divorces anymore either; because nobody really wants to be cut in two!

Jesus fulfilled this element as well when He went to the cross. In fact, He became the slaughtered lamb. He was stretched out on the cross, His blood was shed, He gave His life so that we could become one with Him and one with one another.

In marriage, we surrender our lives so that we can become "one"

Matthew 19:3-9
> *He answered, "Have you not read that he who created them from the beginning made them male and female, and said, 'For this reason a man shall leave his father and his mother and to be joined to his wife, and the two shall become one flesh? So they are no longer two but one flesh. What therefore God has joined together, let not man put asunder."*

This is what is meant by "one flesh". They have died to self to become one.

In the above diagram, we see 2 lines. If you joined the 2 lines at the top and bottom, you suddenly have a rectangle. The 2 separate lines were changed by being joined together.

Now let's just imagine that the 2 lines represent 2 individual people, a man and a woman, (looking slim and trim I might add). When they enter the covenant of marriage, they become one new entity, in fact a new " family" is born in the Kingdom of God and here upon earth. Just as you can no longer identify the separate lines because they are a new entity, so the 2 separate people are now a new entity, "one flesh".

You may ask where blood is shed in a marriage covenant. Well blood has been designed by God to be shed in the marriage covenant, when a man and woman come together and have intercourse for the first time. The woman's hymen is broken and blood is shed. Now there is no other reason for that to be done, I believe, that God has given us a sign to say "there is a covenant that has been made, and it's been sealed in the shedding of blood, even in our marriage covenant."

4. Exchanging Their Wealth - The Terms Of Agreement
The next step would be to discuss the terms of covenant which were simply this; all that I have is yours, all that you have is mine. All their assets and all their liabilities would be added together and what's yours is mine, what's mine is yours. We need to have the spirit of that in our marriage as well; the combined wealth and assets are now "ours".

When Jesus cut covenant with us, we became "joint heirs" with Him.

Rom 8:14-17

> *For all who are led by the Spirit of God are sons of God.*
> *For you did not receive the spirit of slavery to fall back*
> *into fear, but you have received the Spirit of sonship.*
> *When we cry, "Abba! Father!" it is the Spirit himself bearing*
> *witness with our spirit that we are children of God, and*
> *if children, then heirs - **heirs of God and fellow heirs***
> ***with Christ**, provided we suffer with hin in order that we*
> *may also be glorified with him.*

Rom 8:31-32

> *What then shall we say to this? If God is for us, who can*
> *be against us? He who did not spare his own Son but gave*
> *him up for us all, will he not also give us all things with*
> *Him.*

In todays marriages, many couples do not understand this covenant principle. They live with a mindset of a contract that says; what's yours is yours, and what's mine is mine. When couples come in for counselling, finance is often one of the main areas that is causing a problem in their marriage. Their approach is, "Now look, I earn my salary and pay in an amount towards the costs, and the rest of that salary is mine. My wife earns a salary and she pays in an amount and the rest of her salary is hers!" The assets I brought into the marriage are mine and any accrual of value upon these assets will remain mine. So we have this battle taking place. The wife says, "at the end of every month, I run out of salary, and I don't have any money for basic needs like toiletries". The husband says "Well, that's your bad luck; what's yours is yours, and what's mine is mine".

But that's not what covenant is. It's what's yours is mine and what's mine is yours. All the assets and liabilities are "ours" to share, Now I know that prenuptial contracts are drawn up where assets are split to protect the wife and family where the husband has business interests. Legally, it is better to have an ANC (ante-nuptial contract) to prevent assets from being attached by creditors in the event of the business running into financial difficulties. But in the spirit of covenant, we are in fact married in "community of property". The heart and spirit of that is important as finance can be a very contentious dividing point in marriage where the spirit of the relationship is based on selfishness.

5. Exchanging Names

Then they would exchange names. When God cut covenant with Abraham his name was Abram, He became Abraham, because the "AH" out of Jehovah was added to his name; and Jehovah became the God of Abraham. This change of name conveys a powerful message to everyone. It confirms that we are now "one". We are now part of Gods family, joint heirs of His righteousness, position and authority.

In Jesus, we who have cut covenant with God become known as Christians; "Followers of Christ". We take on the name of Christ which then declares our union with Him and our position and authority in Him.

When you get married the wife takes on her husband's surname - so there is an exchanging of names which declares, we are "one".

6. Share A Meal / Take Communion Together

Then they would share a meal together and sometimes give one another gifts. Jesus shared a meal with His disciples, as a fullfilment of Passover before His crucifixion.

Mat 26:26

> *Now as they were eating, Jesus took bread, and*
> *blessed and broke it and gave it to the disciples, and said,*
> *"Take, eat; this is my body." And he took a cup, and when*
> *he had given thanks he gave it to them, saying, "Drink of*

*it, all of you, **for this is my blood of the covenant,** which is poured out for many for the forgiveness of sins.*

Jesus urged His disciples to break bread together or as we now know it as "take communion together" in remembrance of the covenant we have through Jesus.

It is very significant when couples take communion together during their wedding ceremony. What they are saying is that even as Jesus gave His life and shed His blood for us symbolized in the bread and wine, so today as we eat this bread and drink this cup together, it signifies that our lives are now surrendered to each other, the old has gone, the new has begun. We are now "one". Even as we are in Christ and He by the holy Spirit is in us, so we are now one in Him through this covenant. This is a powerful unifying declaration to break bread together in your home. At a wedding ceremony everyone usually goes out to share a wedding meal together, present gifts and celebrate the spiritual birth of a new family in God.

7. BUILD A Memorial

Then they would establish a memorial to the covenant they had cut with one another. That could be the planting of a tree; or the building of a big pile of stones.

The memorial that is most important in all of mankind is the Cross. Jesus Christ gave his life on the Cross and that's where he cut covenant. Whenever you see that Cross, all over the world, it is a sign of the covenant that God cut with us through Jesus Christ.

In our family context, one of the signs is our children. Our children are a sign and blessing of the covenant that has been cut between us. Children that are born into a Godly marriage, inherit the blessing of Gods covenant promise. They will live under the covering, protection, favour, peace, joy and grace of being in covenant with

God. They are a testimony to God's blessing of fruitfulness and the passing down of our inheritance in God.

Ps 25:10

> *All the paths of the Lord are steadfast love and faithfulness*
> *for those who keep his covenant and obey his testimonies.*

Ps 25:12

> *Who is the man who fears the Lord?*
> *Him will he instruct in the way that he should choose.*
> *He himself shall abide in prosperity,*
> *and his children shall inherit the land.*
> *The friendship of the Lord is for those who fear him,*
> *and he makes known to them his covenant.*

Ps 128

> *Blessed is everyone who fears the Lord,*
> *who walks in his ways!*
> *You shall eat the fruit of the labor of your hands;*
> *you shall be blessed, and it shall be well with you.*
> *Your wife will be like a fruitful vine*
> *within your house;*
> *your children will be like olive shoots*
> *around your table.*
> *Behold, thus shall the man be blessed*
> *who fears the Lord*

A Ring

Couples wear a ring on their finger as a sign of their covenant commitment and their eternal love for each other. It is a declaration to the world that you are commited in marriage and that your marriage is commited to God to be a reflection of the divine unity of the Godhead and the eternal marriage of Jesus Christ to His Bride, The Church.

So we see how these aspects of covenant were fulfilled by Jesus and are a very significant part of our wedding and marriage covenant today.

Chapter 4

NEW LIFE

So the elements of covenant are sacrifice, but not just sacrifice unto death, but unto resurrection, to something new - a new life that is born. When a man and a woman cut covenant with one another, they "die" to themselves and become one Husband and Wife team that complete one another.

A "New Family" in the Kingdom of God.
As they now surrender to each other in a spirit of humility, as they accept and trust each other, they will live in the peace, joy and blessing of their marriage covenant.

Now with covenant there is a great exchange that takes place. When Christ cut covenant with us he fulfilled all the terms of the steps that we've just discussed.

Firstly, Jesus exchanged his robe of righteousness and for our garments of sin and shame, we received His Grace, anointing and authority to establish the Kingdom of God on earth. In Mark 16 15-18 we are told to *"Go into the world, make disciples, cast out demons, heal the sick, do everything in His name."*

Jesus also exchanged his "abundance" for our "lack". The Word says that, *"Christ has come that we might have life, and life in abundance,"* instead of the lack that we have walked in. We have not just received "a blessing", but in covenant we have been transported into "THE BLESSING", the Abrahamic covenant blessing that is ours through Jesus Christ.

Gal 3:29
> *And if you are Christ's, then you are Abraham's offspring, heirs according to promise.*

Now, in our marriages, because it's a covenant we too have exchanged "all" .

We now choose to honour, encourage and bless each other, imparting the love, peace, joy and hope of The Lord every moment of the day. That is why God has joined you together, so that you can compliment and complete each other and together overcome the challenges you may face but even more important, impart the blessings of the Kingdom of God to those around you.

Unfortunately, many couples do not understand or know the terms and power of covenant. In fact they are deceived into living under the terms of a contract and even operate in " old covenant" principles.

Old vs New Covenant

Now, if I asked you, as Christians today, would you rather be under the new covenant or would you rather be under to old covenant, I guess most of you would say you would rather be under the new covenant. And there's a good reason for saying that, because we sort of know what the old covenant stands for, or do we?. So let's refresh our memories as we look at the differences. Below is a chart comparing the old covenant and the new covenant.

THE OLD COVENANT (Heb 8, Jer 31:31) STONE (OUTWARD)	**THE NEW COVENANT** (2Cor 3:2 & 3) HEARTS (INWARD)
Law	Rom 8:2 Spirit of Life in Christ Jesus
Judgement	Mercy
Rejection - Separation	Acceptance - Unity
Focus on weakness	Cover weaknesses
Sacrifice of works	Grace, Faith, Hope, Love

Now the old covenant was presented to Moses written out on tablets of stone, and placed in the ark. It was the LAW that governed people's lives. It was a list of rules, that were impossible to keep and if you did not adhere to every aspect of the law, you would be separated from God. However, in the the new covenant, in Hebrews 8 and Jeremiah 31:31, God says, *"I'm bringing a new covenant; I'm going to write my law on your hearts."*   It's going to be an inward thing, it's no longer going to be an issue of an outward covenant on tablets of stone, but it's gong to be an inward covenant, governing your behavior from within. Romans 8 described it as *"the law of sin and death"* – instead of that we have a law that's written of our hearts with a desire to please – there's a desire to please the Lord, and there's a desire to please our covenant partner; and it's sealed, empowered in and by the Holy Spirit.

The old covenant based on rules, caused people to fall short as they could not live a perfect, sin-free life. So there was a focus on weaknesses, because you always fell short of fulfilling the law. In Romans 8 we are told, "Because of our weak flesh we could not fulfill the law." As a result of our weakness, we came under judgement. Then to make our way back into acceptance there had to be a sacrifice of works. They did all kinds of penitence but it was an outward thing all the time. They continually had to perform to fulfill all the terms and conditions of the law. They had to earn their acceptance. Even with God they had to earn their acceptance – it was all a ritualistic thing of keeping certain laws.

That is why they continually made animal sacrifices. The law demanded that a pure and spotless lamb had to be sacrificed, blood had to be shed for the forgiveness of sins so they could be made right with God. History records that at Passover about 250 000 lambs were sacrificed by the priests in the temple.

We had an experience of this recently when we went to Israel. We were standing in front of the Wailing Wall on a Saturday. People in our group took out pens to write some notes and some of the people were using their cameras. The next thing a group of soldiers ran up to us with their Uzi's, shouting and pointing at us. We thought someone in our party had at least robbed a bank! Our guide came to our rescue and said, "Put away the pen, you're not allowed to write on the Sabbath," I mean, they were very intense about the situation, you didn't want to argue with them; this was a law and we were breaking it. Every moment of every day, and especially on the Sabbath, you had to fulfill the outward conditions of the law; This meant you had to earn your acceptance, and if you didn't, there was rejection and separation from God.

Now, as opposed to works, performance and continual sacrifice, we have received forgiveness and salvation through the death and shed blood of Jesus once and for all. Our **faith** in Jesus Christ has brought us into **rest**. Faith and rest, instead of works and performance. Instead of judgement, we have acceptance; through Jesus Christ. We have been made sons and daughters of God. There is now acceptance from the Father towards us. Instead of focusing of our weakness, we have now been made righteous and the blood of Jesus covers our weaknesses. Instead of living under a spirit of judgement, now there is grace and mercy! Instead of a sacrifice of works, under the new covenant you offer your life as a living sacrifice. You can read that in Romans 12:1 and 2, *"Present your bodies as a living sacrifice..."* We come to God through faith, and receive grace and mercy from a loving Father. In Him we find rest!.

Now, it's important to understand the two covenants and their consequences because the shocking news is that much of the time we live under the spirit of the old covenant in our marriages. Why? Because there is continual judgement of faults and weaknesses.
- There is no grace.
- There is expection of "performance" - works.
- There is rejection & seperation.

 Remember how I described Lindah – you're no good in this area, you're weak in this area, why can't you change and improve. Until you perform better in every way, I'm not going to love you as much. That causes separation between couples in marriage. As we counsel couples with marriage problems, mostly its about how much they are judging and condemning each other, because they feel their spouse has failed to perform and fulfill certain expectations.

Once again, let me say, we want to be Christians living under the new covenant dispensation, but in our marriages often we resort to the old covenant ways of judgement. Then we expect a sacrifice of works so that we can accept them again– and that causes us to live under a curse instead of God's blessing.

Now here is a very important truth that can change your life.

There can never be relational intimacy where there is a spirit of judgement.

Continual faultfinding, criticism and judgement results in condemnation, rejection and separation. So closeness, trust and intimacy is not going to happen.

We don't want to live our lives under the law - based on the old covenant; we want it based on the new covenant. And so it's really important that in our marriage we come to understand the difference between the spirit of the old covenant and new covenant. We need to extend grace and mercy towards one another; so there is a spirit of approval and acceptance in your marriage. When you understand that covenant is based on a decision to lay down your life, your rights and your independence, and to shower one another with mercy and grace, you inherit the blessing of the union. When we live under this cover of grace and mercy, the kindness released softens out hearts to want to change ungodly attitudes that are up-setting our spouse. Love, peace, joy and prosperity in every area of your lives is the result.

You mean we have to lay down all our rights? Yes! you've got to be prepared to die to yourself; in fact, if you understand covenant - to you die to yourself. The only way we come into a relationship and intimacy with Jesus Christ is that He died that we may come into covenant with him. The Word says that we have to be *"born again"*, Romans 8 says it very clearly, *"even as Jesus died, so we die with him so that we may be resurrected with him unto a new life."* Baptism signifies that the old self/man dies, *it is no longer I that lives, but Christ that lives within me. This is the only way* to come into covenant with Jesus Christ.

And so, as we stand together as husband and wife at the altar and cut covenant, what you're saying is "Lord the old man has died, and now the new lives," we now become "one flesh."

Imagine a beautiful perfume bottle filled with priceless perfume. The perfume can be likened to our love. Love is a precious thing, isn't it? Love is a wonderful gift given by God to unite and bind us together, to bring a sweet aroma into our relationship. Just like perfume, love can be that aroma. Perfume changes the atmosphere causing us to experience romance, gentleness, acceptance, desire and attraction. Covenant love is like that perfume. but it is formed as we both yield to God the master 'perfumer'.

Now if the bottle is broken the precious perfume is spilled and lost.

Treasure the bottle, and you could re-fill it once the perfume has been used.

This is a great analogy for our marriages. People say" I don't feel anything anymore, our love is finished". That's like saying, the perfume is finished. Now we have a choice. Throw away the bottle, but then we will never be able to refill it again or treasure the bottle, care for it, protect it and refill it with that precious perfume. Covenant is like that bottle. It holds and protects the love that first blossomed in our relationship and marriage. When the stresses of life cause that love to wane and the feelings seem distant, this is not the time to throw away and break the covenant. Do this and the precious love is lost forever. But hold onto, cherish and protect the covenant "bottle", and that love can be refilled with godly attributes to once again bring joy and blessing into the marriage.

The Veil Has Been Removed
When Jesus died on the cross, the curtain or veil which separated the inner court or Holy of Holies from the people in the outer court, was supernaturally torn in two. The curse of the law was broken, Mercy triumphed over judgement and we were set free. There would no longer be a focus on the weaknesses of the people which caused continual separation between God and His people. Soon Jesus released the Holy Spirit so that He could live in us and we in Him. We would receive power to live in His love, mercy, grace and compassion towards each other. That which was impossible under the old covenant, was now possible in Him.
So in our marriages, it is time to remove the veil that has separated us. The veil of fault finding and judgement, bondage and curse. You are now empowered to live in mercy and forgiveness, love and gentleness, peace and joy. We just need to surrender our lives, embrace the meaning and empowering of covenant that is now our inheritance.

Covenant Ceremonies For Your Wedding

If you are reading this book and are considering marriage, you may be wondering how you can tangibly express your covenant without splitting a sheep in two and walking between the pieces of flesh!. Obviously the ceremony performed by the marriage officer and the vows that you express to each other, are the invoking of a covenant in the eyes of God and the law of the country.

However there are some ways to visually express this which are very meaningful to the couple and those attending the ceremony. Here are some to consider.

1. Break Bread Together

Couples can share a small piece of bread and drink from the same cup which is directly in accordance with the covenant ceremony we have described in previous chapters. This also embraces the covenant that Jesus cut with us and which He asked us to acknowledge each time we take communion. Couples should feed each other a piece of the bread just as Jesus did for us saying "this symbolizes my body which I lay down for you today, as we both eat of this same bread, I am now in you and you are in me. As we both drink of this cup, I declare that the old is gone and the new life together begins. We now invite the Holy Spirit to unite us into "one flesh" and empower our marriage to be a reflection of the eternal marriage of Jesus Christ to His bride the church." By the way, this is something that couples can do from time to time in their marriage to re dedicate their lives and marriage to God.

2. Salt Ceremony

It was a custom in Hebrew times that men would carry a pouch of salt on their belts. If they wanted to conclude a binding agreement or form of covenant, they would take a pinch of salt from their belts and give it to each other. As they then put the exchanged salt into their belts they would say that even as the salt is now all mixed up with the other salt in their pouch and could never be identified or therefore returned, so their agreement is now forever binding. At your wedding ceremony, after your vows, couples can take two small bottles of salt representing their lives and together pour them into one new larger bottle. The grains in the new bottle are now inseparable and completely one. As the couple does this, they express that even as the salt is now one, so they are now "one".

3. Candle Ceremony

This is also a beautiful expression of the covenant that a couple is making. Light 2 candles in front of the congregation and say to each other. "This candle represents my life, dreams and passions. As we now light one new candle together, may that new flame represent our new life as a couple and burn brightly forever. I now blow out the old candle as the old is gone and the new has begun". The new candle also represents the flame of the Holy Spirit burning in our lives and marriage.

The important thing in these ceremonies is "the heart" in which they are done. While the elements of the above are beautiful and touching, it is the heart of unconditional and sacrificial yielding your lives and marriage for the glory of God that is the key.

In Conclusion

The spirit of life in Christ Jesus has set us free from the law of sin and death. Which spirit will you yield to, which spirit will overshadow your marriage. Living by the terms of a "contract" or old covenant principles, will leave you vulnerable and exposed to the onslaught on the enemy against your marriage and family. It's the reason over 50% of marriages end in divorce, bringing hurt, pain and shame to people's lives, especially the children.
Know and applying "new covenant" principles will cause you to experience the empowering Spirit of Jesus Christ in your marriage, bringing freedom, joy, peace and abundant love and blessings.
The choice is yours.

"Today I have given you the choice between life and death, between blessings and curses. Now I call on heaven and earth to witness the choice you make. Oh, that you would choose life, so that you and your descendants might live! You can make this choice by loving the LORD your God, obeying him, and committing yourself firmly to him. This is the key to your life." (Deuteronomy 30:19-20 NLT)

Notice that the promise is to you and your children.
As we said in the beginning, marriage and family should be heaven on earth, not hell on earth.
It's time to decide that your marriage will be a reflection of the devine unity of the Godhead and the eternal marriage of Jesus Christ to His bride, the church. When you live by and are empowered by the Spirit of the new covenant in Christ, you will experience this blessing.

A Powerful Promise For Your Family

2 Sam 23:4

> *"Is it not my family God has chosen?*
>
> *Yes, he has made an everlasting covenant with me.*
>
> *His agreement is arranged and guaranteed in every detail.*
>
> *He will ensure my safety and success.*

God bless,
Drummond & Lindah Robinson

Other resources by Drummond and Lindah Robinson include:

Courses:
The Anointed Marriage
Ignite your Marriage
Positioned For Blessing
Together Forever
Woman Of Peace
A Woman Beyond Compare
Women of Promise
Rising Above

Books:
Living In God's River Of Mercy (Available in Afrikaans, French & Germ
Men Of Honor (Available in Afrikaans, Portuguese & Dutch)
7 Secrets To Fan The Flame
Captivating your Husband's Heart (Inspired by the Song of Songs)

Booklets:
Living In Your Miracle
The Pearl Of Great Price (Children)
The Reward Of Honour
Two Kingdoms

TO ORDER:
www.familytransformation.org
www.fti-academy.org

CONTACT DETAILS:
Email: info@familytransformation.org
Tel: +2782 653 3188